HELL & BACK

ADAM LAWS & KERRY HARTE

ISBN-13: 979-8375699264
Independently published

CONTENTS

AFFECT DETECTED

Why did you let her affect you so?

She fueled your perpetual paranoia,

purposely pointing to hidden signs,

anything to play with your mind.

To you, she was the twinkle in the sky,

the sun that shall never cease to rise,

just as long as she stayed in your life.

She held a sway over your day,

much to witnesses dismay.

For you, she wielded a witchlike power,

one which grew with every hour.

A seemingly insipid spell,

one that worked far too well.

ANOTHER ROUND

Ding! Ding! Round one.

This rematch is far from done.

He made you act out and be so cruel,

given that, there are no more rules,

only a fire within to withstand

Him since the ruthless ridicule.

I'm at your side, in your corner,

I'll tell you when to jab or jibe,

remember to duck and dive,

slide to the side before He can strike

a blow to provoke you to throw a

more visible and volatile vibe.

Pack those gloves with sturdy steel,

a jab to his jaw will knock him

down to the floor once more,

He may be in your mind,

but you can win this time,

you've seen fate enlist the fist,

so you can go on and endure.

BEYOND BROKEN

Democracy is full of shameful hypocrisy.

Lives are left in tatters, for all except immortal matters.

Mortals must muddle through the mire,

the ashes left by their little fires.

The system is beyond broke, it's a joke.

Why should anyone go on to even vote?

Lives are lost because no one could do their job.

Mental healthcare is certainly in disrepair.

The pandemic perfectly played into their hands,

this problem didn't exist beforehand.

Anyone with a mind can see this grew over time.

These perpetual politicians live for the coup,

it feeds their toxic brew.

They're contently coasting along in singing

their elitist schoolboy song.

Their caustic cause will carry on even if

they're to ever be voted off,

another elitist will do the job.

Corruption is at its very core,

for which there is a cure.

For the mothers, the sons, the near

victims of these scum.

For those who fell because the system

didn't check they're doing so well.

Light a fire under these toxic little liars,

help the underdog reach what they aspire.

To call them green is a little mean,

their abilities have yet to be seen.

BULLSEYE

You formed the bullseye with the paint I provided,

the centre marked the spot,

the cheap shot that would do the job.

It was perfectly placed,

where it could cause the heaviest heartache.

I know it wasn't a premeditated plan,

that much I understand.

I was the fool for furnishing you with the tools,

I knew you could become cruel.

I knew your headspace wasn't the safest place,

that you may weaponize anything I say.

Not because of anything you've done,

you're far from the first one.

I showed you faith,

I provided the paint,

that bullseye was my mistake.

BURDEN

It's a song that seems so sweet,

the soft serenade of "I'm okay."

A gesture that sways them away,

it's simpler to suffer in silence,

in a "durable" defiance.

They have problems of their own,

they don't really want to know.

Others can cope so I'll silently survive,

hoping it doesn't bury me alive.

Secretly wishing they'd asked again,

because I didn't want to burden my friends.

CARRIED CURSE

Sat alone with nothing else on,

my guilt and fault projects

and mixes with a matter gone

far beyond reaching out,

yet meshed with an air of the

universe into the unknown

whereabouts of my own

belonging, I'll die and go to

hell for this for as long as

I go on to reminisce…

I know by now how tension

entangles and can't reverse

the complexity of a carried curse,

the face of the other

side assures a welcome with

a wink, the blow of a kiss.

<u>CAUGHT UP</u>

Demons beneath us in a tug-of-war

with my wallowing in self-pity,

above them no angels to have it down,

to be modest and fair,

still more demons carrying and

hovering a heavy burden over

via pulling at the brakes should

they choose for me to fall hard

and unheard by the rest of the herd,

to deliver onto down-to-earth

demons even more of my despair

from a rise ridden bout of

breaths caught up on how I had

to go out somehow from somewhere.

CONSCIENCE TO CUSHION

Guilt being a guillotine given the

laps your head of thought go about

and only for it to be lopped off

by the end in going off an edge…

blood in gushing and rushing

for a conscience to cushion for

the silent blast going into ego…

for here and now it all goes,

heads will roll throughout their

thunderous thoughts to only

in turn bewilder themselves…

never see themselves in that

place again, wary of the woes in

wondering will they see tomorrow.

CUSTOMARY

Turn it down a notch for the obnoxious,

they won't be all ears for the stream of

cries reaching into the cracks and crumbling

their paved morals we each agreeably

never really truly walk along unless

you carry feelings via ferry with coins

upon the eyes to take a gamble of where

you're so steadily set to be headed…

they had each betted in the back of their

minds where best you are to be displayed,

consciences climbing clear towards the

end has grown on us to be so customary,

death detaches us once we've come

to break the ice with the colder shoulder

we went to once for it to melt and meet

us halfway there, to be steep and steadied,

knowing so well of the trick of the trade,

just where about shall such of us be buried?

DRASTIC ARE THE DAYS

Drastic are the days in delivering

dishevelled seasons which may overlap

to overstep an unkempt rep in how

grounded our way of wondering

withers yet seemingly works…

see the darkness dwindle in stepping

away once we know for certain

we've met a happily ever after

even given questionable quirks…

then comes the walking in of wintry

spells of wonder where our mentality

erupts having snapped like a frosted

and fickle branch stemming from a fall

since a summer with its heated heartache

hands to us as much of what lurks,

the seediest spring showcases a sunrise

whereby we go about turning over

a new leaf while the life of us is situated

like a shadow to life and its smirks.

ENTHUSIAST

Nerves of steel that had shrunk since

a temperament had fell on harder times,

no longer since taking the wider attempt,

you're within a newfound high for

allowing your soul to slip out on the sly,

going and gone so fast as though to join

that of the piercing and perilous past.

The rain falls but don't go on to believe

for one second it will carry you towards

the scamper of a scary and scheming sky.

Tragedies being trodden over having

wanted for you to wipe your feet on

your way in so nicely as it were asked…

just don't walk in on me here in this

way to see me by the end as an enthusiast.

EVIDENT ENOUGH

Hardly healing, the length of which

a wound goes about in concealing

the lengths discreet between us both

to which I'd go to, I went through,

to have cut across a certain way,

does it even get across the woe?

Going down to show how life drew

the curtain as I acted upon the

manner of a dire and deadly blow…

loved ones, if any, would then be

going about life in living as I did,

each to be going out of their mind?

I held firm a wondrous tragic trip –

having went about the fallible flow,

pursued it in a negative to become

misguided and caught up too late,

given the follow up being evident

enough I had something to show.

FATED DEFEAT

It's true, I don't know what you're even

going through, but I know of the subtle sting,

it strikes your life, it doesn't care if

the timing is not right, what it will bring.

Its poison silently seeps in so deep,

leaving you in a heartbroken heap,

with a "flawless" feeling of fated defeat.

Its venomous vitriol vies for destroying your life,

next it goes for your eyes, dimming the light,

hiding what's in plain sight.

But there is hope, there is an antidote.

You are not alone, talk it out in prayer,

or speak to those who continue to care,

problems are probably enough to be shared.

GONE SO COLD

The substantial substance saw to it for

all of us all being well all along,

drugs in export for a Deity in

dilemma to finetune their

correct charisma having become

carried away and until this day…

for us to carry the conflict out

just to question whatever is there?

He too sees no other way

around an attempt for a worser world,

we are scoffed at, time and

turmoil in tumble in eating away at us,

if we were to distance ourselves

from the feat of forever,

you'd know in time how it could fold…

we're in His universe which has

by now gone so cold.

HEARTILY HOLD

Put something on her conscience,

a mock-up map with no way out,

her humour ends up being heavy,

the way the weight of her ways

nearly saw you out of this world

since being so high-strung –

made out to the rest you were so

heavily involved and in the wrong.

You had fell so deep, enough to

plummet without limit into

a place on the map she was unable

to locate you and heartily hold.

HUNGER

Your search for inner peace,

you treat it like a flavourless feast,

like food that will never fill a hole,

the one deep within your soul.

You hunger for something that is already there,

but you're always looking elsewhere.

You're surrounded by sweet treats,

the perfect way to end any meal,

but you just see lemon without the ade,

never adding sugar to improve the taste.

Life doesn't provide the perfect platter,

sometimes we must make each ingredient matter.

<u>I MAY NAP</u>

I may nap once life runs shorter than thought,

my soul withdrawn for death to deposit,

the so-called God during interrogation,

'so what on earth was it?'

I may nap, a dream forbidden and hidden,

nowhere to be seen since my life was mapped,

it was simply because she played with

my heart which saw its strings via

being strung along and taken

too far for to be snipped, I had snapped.

JURY OF JEERS

Never again will I generate a jury of jeers,

slowly paying for it since being

in the air of arrears… my head in

the clouds having rented romance

just a floor above us all…

to reach a new high towards heaven,

it must be hell downstairs for me

to take a plunge to explore something

so newfound just to amass to a fall.

<u>LET IT REST</u>

Ends will be met once you've

felt you've reached the end…

veins follow suit in no longer

supplying said circulation

driving you out of this world,

gone too soon since going

around and beyond a bend…

cries which chose to shoot for

the skies given the tally of

trembling tripped out tries,

wearing thin as a burden

as opposed to being blessed,

it all ends here this time when

the headboard is set in stone

in no longer relaying nightmares,

only suggests you let it rest.

MAJESTIC CURSES

I feel so sickly,

deep on the inside

where blood once

was flowing so

rhythmic now no

longer wants to reside,

but to be hiding out,

no longer in the flesh,

here I hover so

ghostlike in

riding it all out,

majestic curses have

my blood flow

and myself reach

out to divide,

death never harbours

a thing called doubt,

so be it, this is

how I had died.

<u>SKIN AKIN</u>

I sent you away when you hurt me that day,

I probably should have stayed,

you were spiralling into a deadly, dark cave.

But I fear, I rarely let anyone near.

I'm a woman of many masks.

Which one do I wear?

It depends on who asks.

I go to immeasurable lengths

to present myself with steely strength.

To some, I appeared like an exterminator,

they nicknamed me the Terminator.

When a pin pricks my skin,

I don't seem to bleed,

but my insides reel.

Wearing a mask, it's a delicate art,

one that fell apart when you reached my heart.

There's a price to be paid in knowing me this way,

I banished you back from where you came

because you caused me pain.

SOARING SORROW

Life on a halted haze for all of

whom involved stood down so below,

and little do they even know

how in her mind they had gathered

with a bombardment of stones

to pick up and go on to throw…

to corner her in going out of

this world from a shambled window

made to feel she has no place

else to go… other than floors down

to be met with what lies beneath

and below… 'well, to hell with her,'

they'd ongoingly go,

the light can only from herein

carry about the shift of her shadow,

no one of reason are able to

rescue her from hell breaking loose

as she grows so heavy within her sorrow.

TAKEN SIDES

I'm going to be on the level with you,

the scales, they're still slanted, still askew,

our friendship isn't fully renewed.

The weight of what was weighs heavy in my head,

a sense of foreboding, a sense of dread.

My heart holds hope that the scales shall rise,

that you and I will see eye to eye.

But I know a demon resides inside your mind,

he is callously cruel, especially to my kind,

those who don't reside within your mind.

He has an unparalleled presence,

powering a poisonous paranoia.

You seem to silence him with ale, to no avail,

that just frees him to reign in this domain.

He causes nothing but pain to those who know your name.

With time, my scale will rise to a levelled-out height,

where we were once at each other's side.

THE CONFESSION

I was still there when you thought I didn't care.

You were blocked on all but one line,

I had to make sure you were fine.

You were buried beneath a beast of a struggle,

burdened by a trouble,

one that couldn't be solved by a cuddle.

That bloody deathly dark,

it blinded you to a helpful heart.

It brought out a misplaced hate,

an inner rage that forced me away.

THOSE ABOARD

Going out the way you did lingers

in our minds the way an anchor

brings a ship to a halt…

you left us joyous times,

yes, collected within a

memory though something

was clearly at fault.

Some of which always come

to us with silenced surprise,

we're still here, and just for you,

staying afloat without you

despite the depth you

felt beneath… we'll be here to

row away the reminders

of how you dove into the time

it took for you to have touched

upon a reflection on the surface,

sensing you had no self-belief.

THROUGHOUT

Profuse in dripping out a set of

sweat to succumb to what was once set

in its ways given the here and then,

never within the normality of now…

blood leaving you since and seeing

to your departure throughout,

a tug-of-war fluctuating the score

about your head and where it

was last seen, somewhere they've

never even been to wean you

off the woman you can't seem

to go a day in living without.

<u>TO BE FAIR</u>

A silent prayer to be fair,

to never cease to care,

to continue to be there,

to remember you're failing to fare,

that these moments are rare.

But I feel like a pot on a hob,

the one no one turned off.

My body begins to burn,

my insides insidiously churn.

My blood boils, I need to recoil,

I must scream, let off the steam,

to give you a piece of my mind,

to be unknowing, but unkind.

But that's not fair,

you need a friend who cares.

So, I'll say another prayer,

a hope to be fair, to care,

to continue to be there,

these moments are rare.

UNSTEADILY SUCCUMB

It's a piece of cake I was told,

the slicing would go in my favour –

the voices told me to go and

join them in a place promising

I'd meet a so-called saviour…

probably raving about it and

waving goodbye to what in

turn I may have become…

taken out of place given a God

ridden pace… prevention given

prayer wasn't even there…

I may too have gone out of my

way out of this world having

been one to unsteadily succumb.

<u>WITHIN</u>

Fraught with the thought that I could do more,

that there's something I could say before it's too late.

But you're trapped in a barbaric bubble,

that's inflated by your troubles,

to see such come back down to earth is a wait.

I'm certain the shine of its sides is leaving you blind,

or perhaps it's distorting your sight.

I have tried to break in,

but the bubble must be burst from within,

it has to be let down gently and just right.

WOKEN WATER

Birthday suits once given as a gift

being slipped into for the final act

where we wish to slip out and away,

addressing only the arduous farce

that is a life left unlived and unfulfilled,

a tub of water won't quite cut it for

the tears shed to sink into the earth

being a bathmat soaked up as

opposition to the sponge of a mind

carrying out an absorption of the

dislocated realm the haters would build,

going out of their way to step on into

and see for themselves the sound

of turmoil splashing over since

it all came out about her, in blood,

she had specifically spilled.